Published By Adam Gilbin

@ Mike Kong

Carnivore Diet:Troubleshooting Guide, Carnivore

Diet and Body Composition Anti-aging Benefits

All Right RESERVED

ISBN 978-87-94477-22-2

TABLE OF CONTENTS

Bacon And Egg Salad Sandwich 1

Turkey Sausage And Egg Muffins 3

Beef Carpaccio With Arugula And Parmesan Shavings ... 5

Prosciutto Crudo With Melon 7

Bacon And Eggs Delight 9

Steak And Avocado Scramble 10

Grilled Chicken Salad With Avocado And Cherry Tomatoes 12

Steak And Mushroom Skewers With Garlic Butter 14

Beef Jerky 15

Bacon Wrapped Asparagus 18

Grilled Rib Eye Steak With Herb Butter 19

Bacon Wrapped Chicken Thighs 22

Bacon And Avocado Breakfast Salad 25

Steak And Eggs 27

Bacon And Egg Breakfast Bowl: 29

- Breakfast Quesadilla 30
- Classic Sausage And Bell Pepper Frittata 31
- Spicy Italian Sausage And Jalapeño Frittata 33
- Egg And Bacon Hash 36
- Breakfast Burrito 38
- Grilled Ribeye Steak With Garlic Butter 39
- Pan Seared Salmon With Lemon Dill Sauce 41
- Bacon And Eggs: 43
- Steak And Eggs 44
- Chicken In Cream Sauce 45
- Bacon & Chicken Patties 46
- Chicken Bone Broth 48
- Easy Honey Dill Pickles 50
- Spicy Baked Salmon With Avocado 52
- Bacon And Egg Casserole 54
- Tuna Tartare With Avocado 56
- Stuffed Eggs With Ham 58

Sausage Stuffed Bell Peppers 59

Keto Breakfast Burrito 61

Bbq Pulled Pork Sandwich With Coleslaw Recipe 62

Beef And Vegetable Stir Fry With Soy Sauce 66

Mini Meatballs 69

Garlic Butter Shrimp Skewers 71

Pan Seared Lamb Chops With Rosemary 74

Sausage And Vegetable Skillet 77

Egg Muffins 79

Turkey Sausage And Egg Breakfast Sandwich 81

Breakfast Hash 83

Chorizo And Roasted Red Pepper Frittata 84

Classic Peppered Beef Jerky Bites 86

Breakfast Burger 89

Breakfast Sausage 90

Ovenbaked Chicken Thighs With Crispy Skin 93

Seared Scallops With Herb Butter 95

Sausage And Egg Muffins: 97

Ground Beef And Egg Skillet.. 98

Garlic & Parmesan Wings 100

Drumsticks.. 102

Rendered Beef Tallow 103

Beef Bone Broth 104

5. Beef And Egg Breakfast Burrito 106

Sausage And Egg Breakfast Pizza 108

Steak And Egg Hash.. 110

Mozzarella And Salami Skewers................................... 112

Crispy Chicken Livers.. 114

Smoked Chicken Salad With Avocado.......................... 116

Egg Muffins With Ham 118

Baconwrapped Jalapeño Poppers 120

Beef Jerky 122

Turkey And Bacon Club Sandwich With Lettuce And Tomato 124

Chili Con Carne With Cheese And Sour Cream............. 126

Lamb Kebab With Tzatziki Sauce And Pita Bread......... 129

Caesar Salad Chicken.. 134

Butter And Garlic Steak 136

Pork Tenderloin With Mustard Crust 138

Bacon And Egg Salad Sandwich

Ingredients:

- 2 slices of whole wheat or white bread
- 2 slices of cooked bacon
- 2 boiled eggs, peeled and sliced
- ¼ cup mayonnaise
- 1 tablespoon dijon mustard
- 1 tablespoon chopped fresh chives
- Salt and pepper to taste

Directions:

1. Toast the bread.

2. In a bowl, combine the mayonnaise, mustard, chives, salt, and pepper.
3. Slice the eggs and bacon, and add them to the bowl.
4. Mix until everything is evenly coated.
5. Spread the mixture on the toast.
6. Serve the Bacon and Egg Salad Sandwich.

Turkey Sausage And Egg Muffins

Ingredients:

- 1 cup shredded sharp cheddar cheese

- 1 teaspoon dried oregano

- ½ teaspoon garlic powder

- ¼ teaspoon black pepper

- 2 cups cooked turkey sausage, crumbled

- 3 large eggs

- ¼ cup skim milk

- 6 English muffins, split and lightly toasted

Directions:

1. Preheat oven to 350°F. Grease a 12cup muffin tin with nonstick cooking spray.

2. In a large bowl, whisk together eggs, milk, cheddar cheese, oregano, garlic powder and black pepper.
3. Divide sausage evenly among the muffin cups.
4. Pour egg mixture over sausage.
5. Top each muffin cup with a split and toasted English muffin.
6. Bake for 1820 minutes until muffins are lightly golden and eggs are set.
7. Serve warm. Enjoy!

Beef Carpaccio With Arugula And Parmesan Shavings

Ingredients:

- 50 g parmesan shavings
- Juice of 1 lemon
- Extra virgin olive oil
- 400 g quality beef (preferably tenderloin)
- 100 g fresh arugula
- Salt and freshly
- ground black pepper

Directions:

1. Place the beef in the freezer for about 3040 minutes to make it easier to slice.

2. Meanwhile, wash and dry the arugula well. Take the beef from the freezer and slice it as thinly as possible with a sharp knife.
3. Spread the meat slices on a serving plate in an even layer.
4. Season the meat with lemon juice, extra virgin olive oil, salt, and freshly ground black pepper. Sprinkle the arugula over the beef.
5. Add parmesan shavings on top of the Carpaccio. Serve immediately as an appetizer or light main course.

Prosciutto Crudo With Melon

Ingredients:

- 200 g of prosciutto crudo (preferably of good quality)
- 1 ripe melon
- Fresh mint leaves (optional)

Directions:

1. Cut the melon in half, remove the seeds, and cut the flesh into slices or cubes, depending on your preference.
2. Arrange the prosciutto on a serving platter. Accompany the ham with the melon slices or cubes.
3. If you wish, you can garnish the dish with a few fresh mint leaves to add a touch of

freshness. Serve as an appetizer or as part of a summer buffet.

Bacon And Eggs Delight

Ingredients:

- 24 eggs
- 46 strips of bacon
- Salt and pepper to taste

Directions:

1. In a skillet over medium heat, cook the bacon until crispy. Remove the bacon from the skillet and set it aside.
2. Crack the eggs into the same skillet and cook them to your preferred doneness (e.g., sunnyside up or overeasy). Season with salt and pepper.
3. Serve the eggs alongside the crispy bacon, and enjoy your delightful Bacon and Eggs breakfast!

Steak And Avocado Scramble

Ingredients:

- 23 eggs

- 1 ripe avocado, diced

- 8 oz tender steak slices (e.g., sirloin or ribeye)

- Salt and pepper to taste

Directions:

1. In a skillet over medium high heat, cook the steak slices to your preferred doneness. Season with salt and pepper.
2. While the steak is cooking, whisk the eggs in a bowl and pour them into the skillet with the steak.
3. Scramble the eggs with the steak until fully cooked.

4. Remove from heat and mix in the diced avocado.
5. Serve your Steak and Avocado Scramble warm and enjoy the delicious combination of flavors!

Grilled Chicken Salad With Avocado And Cherry Tomatoes

Ingredients:

- 1/4 cup red onion, thinly sliced
- 1/4 cup chopped fresh cilantro
- 1 lime, juiced
- 2 tablespoons olive oil
- 2 boneless, skinless chicken breasts
- Salt and pepper
- Olive oil
- 6 cups mixed greens
- 1 avocado, diced
- 1 cup cherry tomatoes, halved

- Salt and pepper to taste

Directions:

1. Preheat the grill to medium high heat.
2. Season chicken breasts with salt and pepper, and drizzle with olive oil.
3. Grill chicken for 67 minutes per side, or until cooked through. Let rest for 5 minutes, then slice into thin strips.
4. In a large bowl, combine mixed greens, diced avocado, cherry tomatoes, red onion, and cilantro.
5. In a small bowl, whisk together lime juice, olive oil, salt, and pepper.
6. Drizzle dressing over salad and toss to combine.
7. Divide salad among plates and top with sliced chicken.
8. Enjoy your delicious grilled chicken salad with avocado and cherry tomatoes!

Steak And Mushroom Skewers With Garlic Butter

Ingredients:

- 2 tablespoons fresh parsley, chopped
- 1 teaspoon salt
- 1/2 teaspoon black pepper
- 4 tablespoons unsalted butter, melted
- 1 1/2 pounds sirloin steak, cut into 1inch cubes
- 8 ounces mushrooms, cleaned and trimmed
- 1/4 cup olive oil
- 2 cloves garlic, minced

Directions:

1. Preheat the grill to medium high heat.
2. Thread the steak and mushrooms onto skewers, alternating between the two.
3. In a small bowl, mix together the olive oil, minced garlic, parsley, salt, and black pepper.
4. Brush the skewers with the olive oil mixture, making sure to coat all sides.
5. Grill the skewers for 68 minutes, turning occasionally, until the steak is cooked to your desired doneness.
6. In a separate small bowl, melt the butter in the microwave or on the stovetop.
7. Brush the garlic butter over the cooked skewers before serving.
8. Enjoy your delicious Steak and Mushroom Skewers with Garlic Butter, a perfect addition to any carnivore diet cookbook!

Beef Jerky

Ingredients:

- 1 tbsp. apple cider vinegar
- 1 tsp. onion powder
- 1 tsp. garlic powder
- Salt and pepper
- 1 lb. beef, sliced thinly against the grain
- 1/4 cup coconut aminos (or soy sauce)
- 1 tbsp. liquid smoke

Directions:

1. Mix together the coconut aminos, liquid smoke, apple cider vinegar, onion powder, garlic powder, salt, and pepper in a bowl.
2. Put the sliced beef to a small bowl and toss to coat.
3. Marinate the beef in the fridge for at least 2 hours (or overnight for a stronger flavor).

4. Preheat the oven to 175°F (80°C).
5. Line a baking sheet with parchment paper and place the beef slices on top, making sure they don't touch.
6. Bake the beef slices for 46 hours, or until dry and chewy.
7. Store the beef jerky in an airtight container at room temperature for up to 2 weeks.

Bacon Wrapped Asparagus

Ingredients:

- 1 bunch of asparagus

- 68 slices of bacon

- Salt and pepper

Directions:

1. Preheat the oven to 400°F (200°C).
2. Remove the woody ends of the asparagus by trimming and wash them.
3. Cut the bacon slices in half.
4. Wrap each asparagus spear with a halfslice of bacon and place them on a baking sheet.
5. Season with salt and pepper.
6. Bake for about 1520 minutes, or until the bacon is cooked through and the asparagus is tender. erve hot.

Grilled Rib Eye Steak With Herb Butter

Ingredients:

- 4 tablespoons unsalted butter, softened
- 2 cloves garlic, minced
- 1 tablespoon fresh parsley, chopped
- 2 Rib eye steaks (about 1 inch thick)
- Salt and pepper (to taste)
- 1 tablespoon fresh thyme leaves, chopped

Directions:

1. Heat up your grill to a high setting. To avoid sticking, make sure the grates are clean and lubricated.
2. Take the rib eye steaks out of the fridge, and then give them 30 minutes to come to room

temperature. They will be able to cook more evenly as a result.

3. Prepare the herb butter while the steaks are resting. The softened butter, minced garlic, parsley, and thyme are all combined in a small bowl. All the components should be thoroughly combined.
4. On both sides, liberally salt and pepper the ribeye steaks. Spread the seasoning evenly throughout the meat.
5. The steaks should be placed on the heating grill. Without turning them, cook them for around 45 minutes on the first side. You'll get a beautiful sear from this.
6. The steaks should be cooked for an additional 45 minutes on the other side after being turned after 4–5 minutes. You will receive a mediumrare doneness as a result. Depending on the degree of doneness you choose, alter the cooking time.

7. Remove the steaks from the grill when they are done to your liking and place them on a chopping board. Give them about five minutes to recover. This keeps the meat soft and nobles the juices to be redistributed.
8. Take the herb butter mixture and divide it in half while the steaks are resting. Each steak should have a tablespoon of the herb butter on top, which you should let melt and flavor the meat with.
9. Slice the rib eye steaks thickly against the grain after the resting period. This will make it more palatable and assure softness.

Bacon Wrapped Chicken Thighs

Ingredients:

- 2 tablespoons olive oil
- 2 teaspoons paprika
- 1 teaspoon garlic powder
- 1 teaspoon dried thyme
- 4 boneless, skinless chicken thighs
- 8 slices of bacon
- Salt and pepper to taste

Directions:

1. Turn on the oven to 400 °F (200 °C).
2. Combine the paprika, garlic powder, dried thyme, salt, and pepper in a small bowl. Mix thoroughly.

3. On a chopping board, arrange the chicken thighs flat. Each chicken thigh should have the spice mixture uniformly distributed on both sides.
4. Each chicken thigh should have two bacon slices wrapped around it. The ends should be fastened with toothpicks. With the remaining chicken thighs, repeat the process.
5. In a skillet that is oven safe, heat the olive oil over medium high heat.

6. Add the bacon wrapped chicken thighs, seam side down, to the hot oil. The bacon should be seared for two to three minutes on each side, or until browned.
7. When the chicken is cooked through and the internal temperature reaches 165°F (75°C), place the pan in the preheated oven and bake for about 1520 minutes.

8. Using oven mitts, carefully remove the pan from the oven; the handle will be hot. Before serving, give the chicken thighs some time to rest.

Bacon And Avocado Breakfast Salad

Ingredients:

- 2 cups mixed salad greens

- 2 boiled eggs, sliced

- Cherry tomatoes, halved

- Salt and pepper to taste

- 4 strips of bacon, cooked and crumbled

- 1 avocado, sliced

- Optional: salad dressing of your choice

Directions:

1. In a large salad bowl, combine the mixed greens, cherry tomatoes, and sliced boiled eggs.

2. Add the sliced avocado on top.
3. Sprinkle the crumbled bacon over the salad.
4. Season with salt and pepper to taste.
5. If desired, drizzle your favorite salad dressing over the salad.
6. Toss gently to combine all the Ingredients:.
7. Serve the bacon and avocado breakfast salad as a refreshing and nutritious meal.

Steak And Eggs

Ingredients:

- 1 medium sized steak (such as ribeye or sirloin)
- 2 eggs
- Salt and pepper to taste
- Cooking oil or butter for greasing the pan

Directions:

1. Season the steak with salt and pepper on both sides.
2. Heat a skillet or grill pan over medium high heat and grease it with cooking oil or butter.
3. Cook the steak according to your preferred doneness (e.g., 34 minutes per side for medium rare).
4. While the steak is resting, prepare the eggs.

5. In a separate nonstick skillet, cook the eggs sunnysideup or according to your preference.
6. Transfer the cooked steak and eggs to a plate and serve together as a hearty breakfast.

Bacon And Egg Breakfast Bowl:

Ingredients:

- 1/2 cup cooked quinoa or rice
- 1/4 cup shredded cheese
- Salsa, for topping (optional)
- 2 eggs, scrambled
- 4 slices of bacon, cooked

Directions:

1. Heat a skillet over medium heat.
2. Add the eggs to the skillet and scramble until done.
3. Place the cooked quinoa or rice in a bowl.
4. Top with the scrambled eggs, bacon, and shredded cheese.
5. Serve with your favorite salsa, if desired.

Breakfast Quesadilla

Ingredients:

- 2 flour tortillas

- 1/2 cup shredded cheese

- Salsa, for topping (optional)

- 2 eggs, scrambled

Directions:

1. Heat a skillet over medium heat.
2. Add the eggs to the skillet and scramble until done.

Classic Sausage And Bell Pepper Frittata

Ingredients:

- Farm fresh eggs (as many as desired)

- Salt and pepper to taste

- Olive oil or butter for cooking

- Carnivore friendly sausages (e.g., pork or beef), sliced

- Fresh bell peppers (assorted colors), thinly sliced

Directions:

1. Preheat the oven to 375°F (190°C).
2. In an oven safe skillet, heat olive oil or butter over medium heat.
3. Add the sliced sausages to the skillet and cook until they are browned and fully cooked.

Remove the sausages from the skillet and set them aside.
4. In the same skillet, add the thinly sliced bell peppers and sauté until they are tender and slightly caramelized.
5. In a bowl, beat the farmfresh eggs and season them with salt and pepper.
6. Pour the beaten eggs over the sautéed peppers in the skillet, making sure the vegetables are evenly distributed.
7. Arrange the cooked sausages on top of the eggs in the skillet.
8. Transfer the skillet to the preheated oven and bake for approximately 1520 minutes or until the frittata is set and slightly golden on top.
9. Remove the Sausage and Pepper Frittata from the oven, let it cool slightly, and slice it into wedges.
10. Serve the classic Sausage and Bell Pepper Frittata warm, savoring the delightful

combination of savory sausages and colorful peppers in each mouthwatering bite.

Spicy Italian Sausage And Jalapeño Frittata

Ingredients:

- Farm fresh eggs (as many as desired)

- Salt and pepper to taste

- Spicy Italian sausages, casings removed and crumbled

- Fresh jalapeño peppers, thinly sliced (seeds removed for milder heat)

- Olive oil or butter for cooking

Directions:

1. Preheat the oven to 375°F (190°C).
2. In an oven safe skillet, heat olive oil or butter over medium heat.

3. Add the crumbled spicy Italian sausages to the skillet and cook until they are browned and fully cooked. Remove the sausages from the skillet and set them aside.
4. In the same skillet, add the thinly sliced jalapeño peppers and sauté until they are tender and slightly charred.
5. In a bowl, beat the farm fresh eggs and season them with salt and pepper.
6. Pour the beaten eggs over the sautéed jalapeño peppers in the skillet, making sure the vegetables are evenly distributed.
7. Arrange the cooked spicy Italian sausages on top of the eggs in the skillet.
8. Transfer the skillet to the preheated oven and bake for approximately 1520 minutes or until the frittata is set and slightly golden on top.
9. Remove the Spicy Italian Sausage and Jalapeño Frittata from the oven, let it cool slightly, and slice it into wedges.

10. Serve the zesty and flavorful frittata warm, enjoying the delightful combination of spicy sausages and jalapeño peppers in each delectable bite.
11. Layer the scrambled eggs and cheese on top of the tortilla.
12. Place the other tortilla over the top.
13. Grill for 2 minutes per side or until the tortilla is lightly browned and the cheese is melted.
14. Serve with your favorite salsa, if desired.

Egg And Bacon Hash

Ingredients:

- 2 diced potatoes

- 2 diced bell peppers

- 4 eggs

- 4 slices of bacon

- 2 tablespoons of butter

- 1 diced onion

- Salt and pepper to taste

Directions:

1. Inside a large pan over medium heat, fry the bacon until it is crisp. To drain, place aside on a paper towel.

2. In the same skillet, melt the butter and add the onion, potatoes, and bell peppers. The veggies should be cooked for around 10 minutes, stirring once or twice.
3. Push the vegetables to the side of the skillet and crack the eggs into the empty space. Sprinkle with salt and pepper.
4. Cook until the eggs are cooked to your desired doneness.
5. Add the bacon back to the skillet and mix everything together.
6. Serve and enjoy.

Breakfast Burrito

Ingredients:

- 1 cup of cooked black beans
- 4 eggs
- 4 flour tortillas
- 2 cups of grated cheese
- 2 tablespoons of olive oil
- 1/2 diced onion
- 1/2 diced bell pepper
- 1 diced jalapeno
- Salt and pepper to taste

Directions:

1. Add the olive oil to a big pan and heat it up gently. Add the onion, bell pepper, and jalapeno and cook for about 5 minutes until the vegetables are softened.
2. Add the black beans and cook for another 2 minutes.
3. Push the vegetables to the side of the skillet and crack the eggs into the empty space. Sprinkle with salt and pepper.
4. Cook until the eggs are cooked to your desired doneness.
5. Place a tortilla on a plate and top with the egg and vegetable mixture, cheese, and any other desired toppings.
6. Fold up the burrito and enjoy.

Grilled Ribeye Steak With Garlic Butter

Ingredients:

- 2 cloves garlic, minced

- Fresh parsley, chopped (for garnish)
- 1 rib eye steak (8 oz)
- Salt and pepper to taste
- 2 tablespoons unsalted butter, softened

Directions:

1. Preheat the grill to high heat.
2. Season the rib eye steak generously with salt and pepper on both sides.
3. In a small bowl, mix the softened butter and minced garlic.
4. Grill the steak for about 45 minutes per side for medium are, or adjust the cooking time to your desired doneness.
5. Take the steak off the grill and give it some time to rest.
6. Add some garlic butter and fresh parsley on top of the steak.

Pan Seared Salmon With Lemon Dill Sauce

Ingredients:

- 2 tablespoons unsalted butter

- 1 tablespoon fresh dill, chopped

- Juice of half a lemon

- 1 salmon fillet (6 oz)

- Salt and pepper to taste

- 1 tablespoon olive oil

Directions:

1. Season the salmon fillet with salt and pepper on both sides.
2. Melt the butter and oil in a clean skillet over mediumhigh heat.

3. Place the salmon fillet in the hot skillet, skin side down.
4. Cook for about 45 minutes on each side until the skin is crispy and the flesh is cooked through.
5. While the salmon is cooking, prepare the lemon dill sauce by combining chopped dill and lemon juice in a small bowl.
6. Serve the salmon with a drizzle of lemon dill sauce.

Bacon And Eggs:

Ingredients:

- 4 strips of bacon

- 2 large eggs

- Salt and pepper to taste

Directions:

1. In a skillet, cook the bacon over medium heat until crispy.
2. Remove from the skillet and set aside.
3. Keep the bacon fat in the skillet and crack the eggs into it.
4. Cook the eggs to your desired level of doneness, seasoning with salt and pepper.
5. Serve the eggs with the crispy bacon.

Steak And Eggs

Ingredients:

- 2 large eggs

- Salt and pepper to taste

- 1 rib eye steak

Directions:

1. Preheat a grill or skillet to high heat.
2. Season the ribeye steak with salt and pepper.
3. Cook the steak on the grill or skillet to your desired level of doneness.
4. While the steak rests, cook the eggs in a separate skillet to your liking.
5. Serve the steak and eggs together.

Chicken In Cream Sauce

Ingredients:

- 1 tablespoon butter

- 1 liter milk, warm

- 2 cups onion, chopped

- 1 chicken breast

- Sea salt & black pepper to taste

- 1 tablespoon olive oil

- 2 tablespoons ginger & garlic paste

Directions:

1. Remove fat from your chicken breast before seasoning it with salt and pepper.

2. Get out a large pan and place it over high heat. Heat your oil and butter together, and add in the breast. Brown well.
3. Add in four cups of milk, and mix well. Cover and cook for twenty minutes, and turn halfway through.
4. Remove it from the pan and then add the onion, ginger and garlic paste. Allow it broil for ten minutes, and then add the rest of the milk and beat it all in a blender.
5. Cut the meat into thin slices, and then return it to the pan with the sauce.
6. Bring it to heat, and then serve warm.

Bacon & Chicken Patties

Ingredients:

- 1 egg, whisked

- Sea salt & black pepper to taste

- 1 tablespoon garlic powder

- 1 lb. Minced chicken

- 2 bacon slices, cooked & crumbled

Directions:

1. Start by heating your oven to 400. Get out a bowl and mix all Ingredients: together until smooth. If chunky, add it to a food processor to blend until smooth.
2. Form your patties about a half inch thick. You should be able to make ten to twelve, and then get out a tray.
3. Cover it in foil and lay out your patties. Cook for twenty minutes, and then allow them to cool before serving.

Chicken Bone Broth

Ingredients:

- 1 small celeriac, peeled and coarsely chopped
- 2 carrots, coarsely chopped
- 3 or 4 bay leaves
- 16 cups water
- 1 tablespoon chopped fresh parsley
- 1 whole chicken (3 to 4 pounds)
- 8 to 10 chicken feet
- 2 to 3 chicken heads (optional)
- 1 teaspoon salt, plus more to taste

Directions:

1. Place the chicken in a 6quart slow cooker and add the chicken feet, chicken heads (if using), celeriac, carrots, and bay leaves.
2. Pour the water over all. Cover and cook on low for 24 hours, adding the parsley and salt the last 30 minutes of cooking.
3. Strain the broth through a finemesh strainer; discard the solids. If desired, season to taste with additional salt.
4. Let the broth cool. Pour the broth into clean glass jars. Fasten the lids and store in the refrigerator for up to 7 days or in the freezer for up to 1 year.

Easy Honey Dill Pickles

Ingredients:

- ¼ cup honey

- 1 tablespoon kosher salt

- 2 sprigs fresh dill

- 5 pickling cucumbers

- ½ cup white vinegar

- ½ cup water

Directions:

1. Thoroughly scrub the cucumbers. Remove the stems and slice off the blossom ends.
2. Cut the cucumbers lengthwise into ½inchthick spears or crosswise into ¼inchthick slices. In a medium saucepan, combine the vinegar,

water, honey, and salt. Bring to a light boil and stir to dissolve the honey.

3. Pack the cucumbers loosely into a sterilized pint canning jar, leaving a ½inch headspace. Add the dill to the jar.
4. Pour the hot vinegar mixture over the cucumbers, maintaining the ½inch headspace. Wipe the jar rim and adjust the lid and screw band.
5. Refrigerate the pickles for at least 24 hours or preferably 1 week for flavor to develop. Store the pickles in the refrigerator for up to 1 month.

Spicy Baked Salmon With Avocado

Ingredients:

- 1 teaspoon smoked paprika
- 1 teaspoon sea salt
- 1 teaspoon ground black pepper
- 1/4 cup olive oil
- 1 medium avocado, diced
- 1 lb salmon fillet
- 1 teaspoon chili powder
- 1 teaspoon garlic powder
- 1 lemon, sliced

Directions:

1. Preheat oven to 425 degrees.
2. Line a baking sheet with parchment paper.
3. In a small bowl, mix together chili powder, garlic powder, smoked paprika, sea salt, and ground black pepper.
4. Place salmon on the parchment paper.
5. Drizzle with olive oil and then season generously with the spice mixture.
6. Bake in preheated oven for 1520 minutes, or until cooked through.
7. Remove from oven and top with diced avocado and lemon slices.
8. Serve with additional lemon slices, if desired. Enjoy!

Bacon And Egg Casserole

Ingredients:

- 1/2 cup of shredded cheese

- 1/2 cup of diced onion

- 1/2 cup of diced bell pepper

- 1/2 cup of diced mushrooms

- 1/4 cup of diced ham (optional)

- 8 slices of bacon

- 6 large eggs

- 1/4 cup of milk

- 1/4 teaspoon of salt

- 1/4 teaspoon of pepper

Directions:

1. Preheat oven to 350°F.
2. Cook bacon in a skillet over medium heat until crispy. Remove bacon from pan and set aside.
3. In a large bowl, whisk together eggs, milk, salt, and pepper.
4. Grease a 9x13inch baking dish. Layer the bacon, cheese, onion, bell pepper, mushrooms, and ham (if using) in the bottom of the dish.
5. Pour egg mixture over the top of the Ingredients: in the dish.
6. Bake in preheated oven for 25 minutes, or until eggs are set. Let cool before serving. Enjoy!

Tuna Tartare With Avocado

Ingredients:

- Toasted sesame seeds (optional)
- Chopped fresh chives or parsley (optional)
- 300 g high quality fresh tuna
- 1 ripe avocado
- Juice of 1 lemon
- Extra virgin olive oil
- Salt and freshly ground black pepper

Directions:

1. Cut the tuna into very small cubes and place them in a bowl.
2. Peel and finely chop the avocado, then add it to the tuna. Squeeze lemon juice over the

tuna and avocado mixture to prevent the avocado from oxidizing and add a touch of freshness.
3. Season with extra virgin olive oil, salt, and freshly ground black pepper. Stir gently to blend the Ingredients:.
4. If desired, you can add toasted sesame seeds for a crunchy note or chopped chives or fresh parsley for a touch of additional color and flavor.
5. Cover the bowl with plastic wrap and let sit in the refrigerator for about 30 minutes to allow the flavors to meld.
6. Transfer the tuna tartare with avocado to individual serving plates and serve as a fresh, light appetizer.

Stuffed Eggs With Ham

Ingredients:

- 2 tablespoons mayonnaise
- 1 teaspoon Dijon mustard
- 1 teaspoon lemon juice
- Salt and freshly ground black pepper
- 6 eggs
- 100 g ham
- Freshly chopped parsley (optional)

Directions:

1. Boil the eggs in salted water for about 10 minutes, then cool them quickly under cold running water.

2. Shell the eggs and cut them in half lengthwise. Remove the yolks and transfer them to a bowl. Finely chop the prosciutto and add it to the yolks.
3. Add the mayonnaise, Dijon mustard, and lemon juice to the yolks and ham.
4. Stir until smooth. Season with salt and freshly ground black pepper, adjusting to your taste.
5. Fill the egg halves with the yolk and ham mixture, using a teaspoon or sac à pooches. If desired, garnish with some chopped fresh parsley for a more eye catching presentation.
6. Arrange the stuffed eggs on a serving platter and serve as an appetizer or as part of a buffet.

Sausage Stuffed Bell Peppers

Ingredients:

- 1 lb ground sausage (pork or beef)

- Salt and pepper to taste

- 4 bell peppers (any color)

Directions:

1. Preheat your oven to 375°F (190°C).
2. Cut the tops off the bell peppers and remove the seeds and membranes.
3. In a skillet over medium high heat, cook the ground sausage until it's fully cooked and crumbled. Season with salt and pepper to taste.
4. Stuff each bell pepper with the cooked sausage, pressing it down gently to fill the pepper.
5. Place the stuffed bell peppers on a baking sheet and bake in the preheated oven for 2025 minutes or until the peppers are tender.
6. Serve the Sausage Stuffed Bell Peppers hot and enjoy the hearty and flavorful meal!

Keto Breakfast Burrito

Ingredients:

- 4 oz cooked ground beef (seasoned to taste)
- 1/4 cup shredded cheddar cheese
- 2 large eggs

Directions:

1. In a bowl, whisk the eggs until well beaten.
2. In a skillet over medium heat, scramble the eggs until fully cooked.
3. Lay a tortilla on a plate and place the scrambled eggs, cooked ground beef, and shredded cheddar cheese in the center.
4. Fold the sides of the tortilla over the filling and roll it up to form a burrito.
5. Serve your Keto Breakfast Burrito warm and enjoy a lowcarb and satisfying breakfast!

BBQ Pulled Pork Sandwich With Coleslaw Recipe

Ingredients:

- 1/2 teaspoon black pepper

- 1/2 cup barbecue sauce

- 1/2 cup apple cider vinegar

- 1/2 cup chicken broth

- 8 hamburger buns

- 1 cup coleslaw

- 3 pounds pork shoulder or butt

- 1 tablespoon smoked paprika

- 1 tablespoon garlic powder

- 1 tablespoon onion powder

- 1 tablespoon brown sugar

- 1 teaspoon salt

For the coleslaw:

- 1/2 teaspoon celery seed

- 1/4 teaspoon salt

- 1/4 teaspoon black pepper

- 1/2 head cabbage, finely shredded

- 1/2 cup mayonnaise

- 2 tablespoons apple cider vinegar

- 1 tablespoon sugar

Directions:

1. Preheat your oven to 300°F (150°C).

2. In a small bowl, combine the smoked paprika, garlic powder, onion powder, brown sugar, salt, and black pepper.
3. Rub the spice mixture over the pork shoulder or butt, making sure to cover it evenly.
4. In a Dutch oven or large ovensafe pot, combine the barbecue sauce, apple cider vinegar, and chicken broth. Add the seasoned pork to the pot.
5. Cover the pot and bake for 34 hours, or until the pork is tender and easily shreds with a fork.
6. Remove the pork from the pot and use two forks to shred it. Mix in some of the juices from the pot to keep the meat moist.
7. To make the coleslaw, mix together the shredded cabbage, mayonnaise, apple cider vinegar, sugar, celery seed, salt, and black pepper in a large bowl.
8. Toast the hamburger buns.

9. To assemble the sandwiches, place a generous amount of pulled pork on the bottom half of each bun. Top with coleslaw, and then place the top half of the bun on top.
10. Serve hot and enjoy!

Beef And Vegetable Stir Fry With Soy Sauce

Ingredients:

- 1inch piece of ginger, peeled and grated

- 1 small onion, sliced

- 2 cups of mixed vegetables (broccoli, bell pepper, snow peas, carrots)

- 2 tbsp. soy sauce

- Salt and pepper to taste

- 1 lb. beef sirloin, sliced thinly against the grain

- 2 tbsp. vegetable oil

- 2 garlic cloves, minced

- Optional: sliced scallions, sesame seeds for garnish

Directions:

1. Heat a large wok or skillet over high heat. Add the vegetable oil and swirl to coat the pan.
2. Add the beef to the wok and cook for 23 minutes, until browned on all sides. Remove the beef from the wok and set aside.
3. In the same wok, add the garlic and ginger and stirfry for 30 seconds until fragrant.
4. Add the onion and stirfry for 12 minutes until slightly softened.
5. Add the mixed vegetables to the wok and stirfry for 23 minutes until they are just tendercrisp.
6. Add the beef back to the wok along with the soy sauce and toss everything together to combine.
7. Season with salt and pepper to taste.
8. Serve hot, garnished with sliced scallions and sesame seeds if desired.

9. Enjoy your delicious beef and vegetable stirfry with soy sauce!

Mini Meatballs

Ingredients:

- 1/4 cup almond flour
- 1 tbsp. dried oregano
- 1 tbsp. dried basil
- 1 tsp. garlic powder
- 1 lb. ground beef
- 1 egg
- Salt and pepper

Directions:

1. Preheat the oven to 375°F (190°C).
2. Mix together the ground beef, egg, almond flour, oregano, basil, garlic powder, salt, and pepper in a mixing bowl.

3. Roll the mixture into little or small meatballs, or about 1 inch in diameter.
4. Place the rolled meatballs on a baking sheet lined with parchment paper.
5. Bake for about 2025 minutes, or until cooked properly.
6. Serve hot.

Garlic Butter Shrimp Skewers

Ingredients:

- 1 tablespoon lemon juice

- 1/2 teaspoon salt

- 1/4 teaspoon black pepper

- Wooden or metal skewers

- 1 pound (450g) large shrimp, peeled and deveined

- 4 tablespoons unsalted butter, melted

- 4 cloves garlic, minced

- 1 tablespoon fresh parsley, chopped

Directions:

1. To avoid burning while grilling, soak wooden skewers in water for around 20 to 30 minutes.
2. Melted butter, minced garlic, parsley, lemon juice, salt, and black pepper should all be combined in a small bowl. To make sure the components are properly combined, stir the mixture well.
3. Heat up the broiler in your oven or the grill to medium high.
4. Each shrimp's head and tail should be pierced before being threaded onto the skewers. To achieve consistent cooking, space out each shrimp slightly.
5. Brush sufficient amounts of the garlic butter mixture on both sides of the shrimp skewers. Make sure to evenly coat them.
6. Place the skewers on the grill or, if using an oven, a broiler pan. If grilling, the shrimp should be cooked for two to three minutes on each side, or until pink and opaque. If broiling,

cook the shrimp for two to three minutes on each side, watching carefully to avoid scorching.

7. Remove the shrimp from the grill or oven once they are fully cooked. Since the skewers could be hot, use caution when handling them.
8. While they are still hot, serve the Garlic Butter Shrimp Skewers right away. If you'd like, you can add more fresh parsley to garnish.

Pan Seared Lamb Chops With Rosemary

Ingredients:

- 2 tablespoons olive oil
- 2 tablespoons fresh rosemary leaves, chopped
- 2 cloves garlic, minced
- 4 lamb chops
- Salt and pepper to taste

Directions:

1. Prepare the oven: After searing the lamb chops, preheat the oven to 400°F (200°C).
2. Lamb chops should be thoroughly seasoned with salt and pepper on both sides after being patted dry with paper towels.

3. Olive oil is added to a big skillet that has been heated to mediumhigh heat. Give the oil a minute or two to warm up.
4. Lamb chops should be seared for 3 to 4 minutes on each side, or until a golden brown crust forms. Place the lamb chops on the heated skillet.
5. While the lamb chops are still in the skillet, sprinkle them with the minced garlic and chopped rosemary leaves. To help the rosemary and garlic stick to the chops, press them onto them.
6. Finish in the oven: Place the preheated oven on the lowest rack and cook the lamb chops for a further 58 minutes, or until they are cooked through to your liking. You should aim for an internal temperature of 145°F (63°C) if you like your lamb chops mediumrare.
7. Rest the lamb chops: When the lamb chops are done to your preference, remove the pan

from the oven and give them a few minutes to rest. Chops that are soft and juicy are produced as a result of the redistribution of juices.

Sausage And Vegetable Skillet

Ingredients:

- 1 zucchini, sliced

- Salt and pepper to taste

- Cooking oil or butter for greasing the pan

- 4 sausages (choose your favorite variety)

- 1 bell pepper, sliced

- 1 small onion, sliced

Directions:

1. Heat a skillet over medium heat and grease it with cooking oil or butter.
2. Add the sausages to the skillet and cook until browned and cooked through.

3. Remove the sausages from the skillet and set them aside.
4. In the same skillet, add the sliced bell pepper, onion, and zucchini.
5. Sauté the vegetables until they are tendercrisp.
6. Slice the cooked sausages and add them back to the skillet.
7. Season with salt and pepper to taste.
8. Stir everything together and cook for an additional minute or two.
9. Serve the sausage and vegetable skillet as a satisfying and flavorful breakfast option.

Egg Muffins

Ingredients:

- 1/4 cup diced onions
- 1/4 cup shredded cheddar cheese
- Salt and pepper to taste
- Cooking oil or butter for greasing the muffin tin
- 6 eggs
- 1/2 cup chopped cooked bacon or ham
- 1/4 cup diced bell peppers

Directions:

1. Preheat the oven to 350°F (175°C) and grease a muffin tin with cooking oil or butter.

2. In a bowl, whisk the eggs until well beaten. Season with salt and pepper.
3. Add the chopped bacon or ham, diced bell peppers, diced onions, and shredded cheddar cheese to the bowl.
4. Mix well to combine.
5. Pour the egg mixture evenly into the greased muffin tin, filling each cup about three quarters full.
6. Bake in the preheated oven for 1520 minutes or until the egg muffins are set and slightly golden on top.
7. Remove from the oven and let them cool for a few minutes.
8. Carefully remove the egg muffins from the tin.
9. Serve the egg muffins as a convenient grabandgo breakfast option or enjoy them warm with a side of fresh vegetables.

Turkey Sausage And Egg Breakfast Sandwich

Ingredients:

- 2 slices of bread

- Butter, for spreading

- 2 eggs, scrambled

- 2 turkey sausage patties, cooked

Directions:

1. Heat a skillet over medium heat.
2. Add the eggs to the skillet and scramble until done.
3. Spread butter on one side of each slice of bread.
4. Place the turkey sausage patties on one slice of bread.
5. Top with the scrambled eggs.

6. Place the other slice of bread on top.
7. Grill the sandwich in the skillet for about 2 minutes per side or until the bread is golden and the cheese is melted.

Breakfast Hash

Ingredients:

- 1/4 cup cooked sausage, diced
- 1/4 cup shredded cheese
- Salsa, for topping (optional)
- 2 eggs, scrambled
- 1/2 cup cooked potatoes, diced

Directions:

1. Heat a skillet over medium heat.
2. Add the potatoes and sausage to the skillet and cook until lightly browned.
3. Add the eggs and scramble until done.
4. Add the cheese and stir until melted.
5. Serve with your favorite salsa, if desired.

Chorizo And Roasted Red Pepper Frittata

Ingredients:

- Farm fresh eggs (as many as desired)

- Salt and pepper to taste

- Olive oil or butter for cooking

- Chorizo sausages, casings removed and crumbled

- Roasted red bell peppers, thinly sliced

Directions:

1. Preheat the oven to 375°F (190°C).
2. In an oven safe skillet, heat olive oil or butter over medium heat.
3. Add the crumbled chorizo sausages to the skillet and cook until they are browned and

fully cooked. Remove the sausages from the skillet and set them aside.
4. In the same skillet, add the thinly sliced roasted red bell peppers and sauté until they are tender and imparting their smoky flavors.
5. In a bowl, beat the farm fresh eggs and season them with salt and pepper.
6. Pour the beaten eggs over the sautéed roasted red bell peppers in the skillet, ensuring even distribution.
7. Arrange the cooked chorizo sausages on top of the eggs in the skillet.
8. Transfer the skillet to the preheated oven and bake for approximately 1520 minutes or until the frittata is set and slightly golden on top.
9. Remove the Chorizo and Roasted Red Pepper Frittata from the oven, let it cool slightly, and slice it into wedges.
10. Serve the vibrant and hearty frittata warm, relishing the combination of bold chorizo and

smoky roasted red peppers in each delectable bite.

Classic Peppered Beef Jerky Bites

Ingredients:

- 1 tablespoon freshly ground black pepper

- 1 teaspoon onion powder

- 1 teaspoon garlic powder

- 1/2 teaspoon sea salt (optional, if not using tamari sauce)

- 1 pound of high quality beef (e.g., top round or flank steak), thinly sliced against the grain

- 1/4 cup coconut amines or tamari sauce

- 1 tablespoon apple cider vinegar

- Pinch of cayenne pepper (optional, for added heat)

Directions:

1. In a bowl, combine the coconut amines or tamari sauce, apple cider vinegar, black pepper, onion powder, garlic powder, sea salt (if using), and cayenne pepper (if desired) to create the marinade.
2. Add the thinly sliced beef to the marinade, ensuring that each piece is evenly coated. Cover the bowl and refrigerate for at least 4 hours or overnight for maximum flavor absorption.
3. Preheat your oven to 175°F (80°C) or the lowest setting possible.
4. Remove the marinated beef slices from the refrigerator and pat them dry with paper towels to remove excess moisture.

5. Arrange the beef slices on a baking sheet lined with parchment paper or a wire rack placed on a baking sheet.
6. Place the baking sheet in the preheated oven and bake the beef slices for 34 hours or until they become firm and dry, but still pliable.
7. Let the beef jerky bites cool completely before storing them in an airtight container for up to two weeks. Enjoy this classic peppered beef jerky as a delectable and protein packed snack.

Breakfast Burger

Ingredients:

- 1 teaspoon of Worcestershire sauce

- 4 slices of bacon

- 4 hamburger buns

- 4 eggs

- 1 pound of ground beef

- 1 teaspoon of garlic powder

- 1 teaspoon of onion powder

- Salt and pepper to taste

Directions:

1. In a large bowl, mix together the ground beef, garlic powder, onion powder, and Worcestershire sauce. Form the mixture into 4 patties.
2. To sauté the bacon, prepare a big pan over moderate temperature. To soak, place aside on a piece of paper.
3. In the same skillet, cook the burgers for about 5 minutes on each side until cooked to your desired doneness.
4. Push the burgers to the side of the skillet and crack the eggs into the empty space. Sprinkle with salt and pepper.
5. Cook until the eggs are cooked to your desired doneness.
6. Place the burgers on the buns and top with a fried egg and bacon. Serve and enjoy.

Breakfast Sausage

Ingredients:

- 1 teaspoon of mustard powder
- 1 teaspoon of fennel seed
- 1 teaspoon of red pepper flakes
- 4 eggs
- 1 pound of ground beef
- 2 teaspoons of garlic powder
- Salt and pepper to taste

Directions:

1. In a large bowl, mix together the ground beef, garlic powder, mustard powder, fennel seed, and red pepper flakes. Form the mixture into 8 patties.
2. In a large skillet, cook the patties for about 5 minutes on each side until cooked through.

3. Push the patties to the side of the skillet and crack the eggs into the empty space. Sprinkle with salt and pepper.
4. Cook until the eggs are cooked to your desired doneness.
5. Serve the patties with the eggs and enjoy.

Ovenbaked Chicken Thighs With Crispy Skin

Ingredients:

- 1 teaspoon garlic powder

- 1 teaspoon onion powder

- 1 tablespoon olive oil

- 4 chicken thighs, bonein and skinon (approximately 1.5 lbs)

- Salt and pepper to taste

- 1 teaspoon smoked paprika

Directions:

1. Preheat the oven to 425°F (220°C).
2. Pat the chicken thighs dry with a paper towel and season them generously with salt,

pepper, smoked paprika, garlic powder, and onion powder.
3. Heat olive oil in an ovensafe skillet over mediumhigh heat.
4. Place the chicken thighs, skin side down, in the hot skillet and cook for about 5 minutes until the skin is crispy and browned.
5. Transfer the skillet to the preheated oven and bake for 2025 minutes until the chicken is cooked through and the internal temperature reaches 165°F (74°C).
6. Allow the chicken to cool for a while before serving.

Seared Scallops With Herb Butter

Ingredients:

- 2 cloves garlic, minced

- 1 tablespoon fresh parsley, chopped

- 1 tablespoon fresh lemon juice

- 8 large scallops

- Salt and pepper to taste

- 2 tablespoons unsalted butter

Directions:

1. Pat the scallops dry with a paper towel and season them with salt and pepper on both sides.
2. In a skillet over mediumhigh heat, melt the butter.

3. When the butter is melted and foamy, add the scallops to the skillet, making sure they are not overcrowded.
4. Sear the scallops for about 23 minutes on each side until they are golden brown and opaque in the center.
5. Remove the scallops from the skillet and set them aside.
6. In the same skillet, add minced garlic and cook for about 1 minute until fragrant.
7. Remove the skillet from the heat and stir in chopped parsley and lemon juice.
8. Drizzle the herb butter over the seared scallops and serve immediately.

Sausage And Egg Muffins:

Ingredients:

- 6 sausage patties

- 6 large eggs

- Salt and pepper to taste

Directions:

1. Preheat the oven to 375°F (190°C).
2. Grease a muffin tin or line with muffin liners.
3. Press one sausage patty into each muffin cup, forming a crust.
4. Crack one egg into each sausage crust.
5. Season with salt and pepper.
6. Bake in the preheated oven for 1520 minutes until the eggs are cooked to your liking.
7. Remove from the oven and let them cool slightly before serving.

Ground Beef And Egg Skillet

Ingredients:

- 4 large eggs

- Salt and pepper to taste

- 1 pound ground beef

- Optional: spices like garlic powder, onion powder, paprika, etc.

Directions:

1. Heat a skillet over medium heat.
2. Add the ground beef to the skillet and cook until browned and cooked through.
3. Season the ground beef with salt, pepper, and any additional spices you prefer.
4. Make four wells in the ground beef and crack one egg into each well.

5. Season the eggs with salt and pepper.
6. Cover the skillet and cook for a few minutes until the eggs reach your desired level of doneness.
7. Serve the ground beef and eggs together in the skillet.

Garlic & Parmesan Wings

Ingredients:

- 1 egg

- ½ teaspoon italian seasoning

- 8 tablespoons butter, melted

- 6 lb. Whole chicken wings

- ½ Cup parmesan cheese

- 1 teaspoon garlic powder

- ¼ teaspoon crushed red pepper

- ¼ teaspoon sea salt

Directions:

1. Heat your oven to 425, and then slice your wings into two sections.
2. Get out a baking sheet and place a metal rack on top. Put your wings on this rack. Cook for fifteen minutes.
3. To make the sauce combine your butter, seasonings, eggs, and cheese in a bowl.
4. Remove them from the oven and flip them. Turn on your broiler and cook for five minutes. Flip again and cook for an additional five minutes.
5. Toss in the sauce, and garnish with cheese before serving.

Drumsticks

Ingredients:

- 2 tablespoons sea salt

- 2 lb. Chicken drumsticks

- ½ Tablespoon coconut oil

- 3 tablespoons gram macula

Directions:

1. Start by turning the oven to 450, and then get out a large baking sheet. Coat with coconut oil.
2. Mix your gram macula with salt and then pat your drumsticks dry before coating them in the mix.
3. Lay them in an even layer on the baking sheet, and bake for forty minutes. Serve warm.

Rendered Beef Tallow

Ingredients:

- 4 pounds raw beef suet, finely chopped

Directions:

1. Put the suet in a slow cooker. Set on low, and cover.
2. Stir the suet every hour to prevent the cracklings (the brown bits) from sticking to the bottom.
3. The suet is rendered when the cracklings float on the surface and are slightly brown.
4. Turn off the slow cooker. Pour the rendered tallow through a cheesecloth into glass jars.
5. When the tallow cools, it will solidify and appear white.

Beef Bone Broth

Ingredients:

- 3 tablespoons chopped peeled celeriac (optional)

- 4 bay leaves

- 2 teaspoons salt, plus more to taste

- 2 long beef trotters (10 to 12 inches), with the tendons along the bone

- 12 cups water

- 2 carrots, coarsely chopped

Directions:

1. Place the trotters in a 6*q*uart slow cooker. Add the water, carrots, celeriac (if using), bay

leaves, and salt. Cover and cook on low for 24 hours.

2. Remove the bones and set aside to cool. Once cool, remove any remaining pieces of tendon and (optional) save for The Saladino Specialty recipe or just to consume on their own (they're a great source of gelatin!). Discard or compost the bare bones.
3. Strain the broth through a finemesh strainer. Keep any remaining tendon, and discard the vegetables and bay leaves. If desired, season the broth with additional salt.
4. Pour the broth into clean glass jars. Fasten the lids and store in the refrigerator for up to 7 days or in the freezer for up to 1 year.

5. Beef And Egg Breakfast Burrito

Ingredients:

- 1 teaspoon Chili Powder

- 1/2 teaspoon Cumin

- 1/2 teaspoon Paprika

- 1/2 teaspoon Onion Powder

- 8 large Flour Tortillas

- 1 cup Shredded Cheese

- 1 pound Ground Beef

- 8 large Eggs

- 2 tablespoons Olive Oil

- 1 teaspoon Salt

- 1 teaspoon Pepper

- 1 teaspoon Garlic Powder

- 1 cup Salsa

Directions:

1. In a large skillet over medium high heat, cook the ground beef until it is no longer pink. Drain off any excess fat.
2. In a medium bowl, whisk together the eggs, olive oil, salt, pepper, garlic powder, chili powder, cumin, paprika, and onion powder.
3. Pour the egg mixture into the skillet with the beef and cook until the eggs are cooked through.
4. Lay out the tortillas and divide the beef and egg mixture evenly among them.
5. Top each tortilla with the cheese and salsa.
6. Roll up the tortillas and enjoy!

Sausage And Egg Breakfast Pizza

Ingredients:

- ½ cup shredded mozzarella cheese
- 2 cooked breakfast sausage links, sliced
- 1 cooked egg, sliced
- 1 premade pizza crust
- ½ cup pizza sauce

Directions:

1. Preheat oven to 375 degrees F.
2. Spread pizza sauce over premade pizza crust.
3. Sprinkle mozzarella cheese over the sauce.
4. Top with sliced cooked breakfast sausage links and egg.
5. Bake for 2025 minutes or until cheese is melted and bubbly.

6. Slice and serve.

Steak And Egg Hash

Ingredients:

- 2 cloves garlic, minced

- 1 teaspoon smoked paprika

- 2 cups cubed cooked steak

- 2 cups diced potatoes

- 4 eggs

- 2 tablespoons olive oil

- 1 small onion, diced

- 1 red bell pepper, diced

- Salt and pepper to taste

Directions:

1. Heat the olive oil in a large skillet over medium high heat.
2. Add the onion, bell pepper, garlic, and smoked paprika, and cook for 45 minutes until the vegetables are tender.
3. Add the steak and potatoes and cook for 5 minutes, stirring occasionally.
4. Make four wells in the mixture and crack an egg into each one.
5. Reduce the heat to medium low and cover the skillet. Cook until the eggs are cooked to your desired doneness, about 5 minutes.
6. Serve the hash warm, with salt and pepper to taste.

Mozzarella And Salami Skewers

Ingredients:

- 1 red bell pepper
- 1 green bell pepper
- 1 red onion
- Olive oil
- Salt and pepper to taste
- 200 g mozzarella cheese
- 100 g salami
- Sprigs of rosemary (optional)

Directions:

1. Cut the mozzarella and salami into cubes of similar size. Cut the peppers and onion into large pieces.
2. Prepare skewers by alternately threading the mozzarella, salami, pepperoni, and onion cubes onto wooden or metal skewers.
3. Brush the skewers with a little olive oil and season with salt and pepper. If you wish, you can also add sprigs of rosemary to further flavor the skewers.
4. Preheat the grill or a nonstick skillet over medium high heat.
5. Cook the skewers for about 5 to 7 minutes on each side, turning them gently, until the mozzarella cheese has melted and they have turned a nice golden color. Remove the skewers from the grill or pan and serve hot.

Crispy Chicken Livers

Ingredients:

- 2 eggs
- Salt and pepper to taste
- Vegetable oil for frying
- 500 g chicken livers
- 100 g of breadcrumbs
- 50 g flour

Directions:

1. Clean and dry the chicken livers, removing any unwanted skin or fatty parts. In a bowl, crack the eggs and beat them with salt and pepper.
2. In a separate dish, mix together the breadcrumbs and flour. Dip the livers first in

the egg mixture and then in the breadcrumbs and flour mixture, making sure to cover them completely.

3. Gently shake the livers to remove excess breadcrumbs. Heat plenty of vegetable oil in a frying pan over medium high heat.
4. Fry the livers in hot oil until golden brown and crisp, turning them occasionally to ensure even cooking. This will take about 5 to 7 minutes.
5. Once cooked, drain them on paper towels to remove excess oil. Serve the crispy chicken livers hot as an appetizer or accompaniment.

Smoked Chicken Salad With Avocado

Ingredients:

- 1 tomato

- 1 cucumber

- Lemon juice

- Olive oil

- Salt and pepper to taste

- 2 smoked chicken breasts

- 2 ripe avocados

- 1 head of lettuce or mixed salad

- Fresh parsley (optional)

Directions:

1. Cut the smoked chicken breast into cubes or strips. Peel and dice the avocados. Wash and cut the lettuce or mixed salad.
2. Dice the tomato and cucumber. In a large bowl, combine the smoked chicken, avocados, lettuce, tomato, and cucumber.
3. Squeeze lemon juice over the salad and season with olive oil, salt, and pepper to taste. Gently mix all Ingredients: until well combined.
4. Add fresh chopped parsley on top of the salad, if desired. Serve smoked chicken salad with avocado fresh and tasty.

Egg Muffins With Ham

Ingredients:

- 6 large eggs

- 1/2 cup diced ham

- Salt and pepper to taste

Directions:

1. Preheat your oven to 350°F (175°C) and grease a muffin tin.
2. In a bowl, whisk the eggs until well combined. Season with salt and pepper.
3. Divide the diced ham evenly among the muffin tin cups.
4. Pour the whisked eggs over the ham in each cup, filling them about 2/3 full.

5. Bake in the preheated oven for 1520 minutes or until the egg muffins are set and lightly golden.
6. Allow the Egg Muffins with Ham to cool slightly before serving. Enjoy these convenient and delicious breakfast treats!

Baconwrapped Jalapeño Poppers

Ingredients:

- 1/2 cup shredded cheddar cheese

- 12 slices of bacon, cut in half

- 12 fresh jalapeño peppers

- 4 oz cream cheese, softened

Directions:

1. Preheat your oven to 375°F (190°C) and line a baking sheet with parchment paper.
2. Cut each jalapeño in half lengthwise and remove the seeds and membranes.
3. In a bowl, mix the softened cream cheese and shredded cheddar cheese until well combined.

4. Fill each jalapeño half with the cheese mixture, smoothing the top.
5. Wrap each stuffed jalapeño with a half slice of bacon, securing it with a toothpick if needed.
6. Place the bacon wrapped jalapeño poppers on the prepared baking sheet.
7. Bake in the preheated oven for 2025 minutes or until the bacon is crispy and the cheese is bubbly.
8. Allow the poppers to cool slightly before serving. Enjoy the delightful heat and flavor of these appetizers!

Beef Jerky

Ingredients:

- 1 teaspoon garlic powder
- 1 teaspoon onion powder
- 1/2 teaspoon black pepper
- 1 lb beef (such as top round or flank steak), thinly sliced against the grain
- 1/4 cup soy sauce (or coconut amines for a gluten free option)
- 2 tablespoons Worcestershire sauce

Directions:

1. In a bowl, mix the soy sauce, Worcestershire sauce, garlic powder, onion powder, and black pepper to create the marinade.

2. Place the thinly sliced beef into a reseal able plastic bag or a shallow dish.
3. Pour the marinade over the beef, making sure all slices are coated. Seal the bag or cover the dish and refrigerate for at least 4 hours or preferably overnight.
4. Preheat your oven to 175°F (80°C) or the lowest temperature setting.
5. Line a baking sheet with parchment paper.
6. Lay the marinated beef slices on the prepared baking sheet, ensuring they are not touching each other.
7. Bake the beef in the preheated oven for 46 hours or until the jerky is dry and chewy but not overly crisp.
8. Allow the Beef Jerky to cool completely before storing it in an airtight container. Enjoy this high protein snack!

Turkey And Bacon Club Sandwich With Lettuce And Tomato

Ingredients:

- 2 tablespoons of mayonnaise

- 2 leaves of lettuce

- 2 slices of tomato

- Salt and pepper to taste

- 8 slices of turkey breast

- 8 slices of cooked bacon

- 4 slices of your preferred bread (sourdough, whole grain, etc.)

Directions:

1. Toast the slices of bread until golden brown and set aside.

2. Wash the lettuce leaves and tomato slices, then pat them dry.
3. Spread mayonnaise on one side of each of the toasted bread slices.
4. Layer the turkey slices on top of the mayonnaise on two of the slices of bread.
5. Add the bacon slices on top of the turkey.
6. Season with salt and pepper to taste.
7. Place a lettuce leaf and a slice of tomato on top of the bacon.
8. Top with the remaining slices of bread, mayonnaise side down.
9. Cut the sandwich in half diagonally and serve immediately.

Chili Con Carne With Cheese And Sour Cream

Ingredients:

- 1 tsp ground cumin

- 1 tsp dried oregano

- 1/2 tsp salt

- 1/4 tsp black pepper

- 1 cup shredded cheddar cheese

- 1/2 cup sour cream

- 2 lbs. ground beef

- 1 large onion, chopped

- 4 cloves garlic, minced

- 1 green bell pepper, diced

- 2 cans (14.5 oz each) diced tomatoes

- 1 can (15 oz) kidney beans, drained and rinsed

- 1 can (6 oz) tomato paste

- 2 tbsp chili powder

Directions:

1. In a large pot or Dutch oven, brown the ground beef over medium heat. Drain off any excess fat.
2. Add the onion, garlic, and green bell pepper to the pot and sauté for 57 minutes, until softened.
3. Add the diced tomatoes, kidney beans, tomato paste, chili powder, cumin, oregano, salt, and black pepper to the pot. Stir to combine.
4. Bring the chili to a simmer and cook for 2025 minutes, until the flavors have melded together.
5. Serve the chili hot, topped with shredded cheddar cheese and a dollop of sour cream.

Lamb Kebab With Tzatziki Sauce And Pita Bread

Ingredients:

For Lamb Kebabs:

- 1 yellow bell pepper, cut into chunks

- 2 cloves garlic, minced

- 2 tablespoons olive oil

- 1 tablespoon dried oregano

- Salt and pepper to taste

- 1 lb lamb meat, cubed

- 1 red onion, cut into chunks

- 1 red bell pepper, cut into chunks

- Metal or bamboo skewers

For Tzatziki Sauce:

- 1 tablespoon chopped fresh dill

- 1 clove garlic, minced

- 1 tablespoon lemon juice

- 1 cup Greek yogurt

- 1/2 cup grated cucumber

- Salt and pepper to taste

For Pita Bread:

- 1/2 cup warm water

- 1/2 cup plain Greek yogurt

- 2 tablespoons olive oil

- 2 cups all purpose flour

- 1 teaspoon salt

- 1 teaspoon sugar

- 1 tablespoon active dry yeast

Directions:

1. To make the lamb kebabs, preheat the grill or grill pan to medium high heat. If using bamboo skewers, soak them in water for at least 30 minutes to prevent burning.
2. In a large bowl, combine cubed lamb, red onion, red bell pepper, yellow bell pepper, minced garlic, olive oil, dried oregano, salt, and pepper. Mix well to coat everything with the spices and oil.
3. Thread the lamb and vegetables onto skewers, alternating between the lamb and veggies.

4. Grill the skewers for about 810 minutes, turning occasionally, until the lamb is cooked through and the vegetables are tender and slightly charred.
5. While the kebabs are cooking, make the tzatziki sauce. In a medium bowl, mix together Greek yogurt, grated cucumber, chopped fresh dill, minced garlic, lemon juice, salt, and pepper. Mix well to combine and set aside.
6. To make the pita bread, combine flour, salt, sugar, and active dry yeast in a large mixing bowl. Add warm water, Greek yogurt, and olive oil. Mix with a wooden spoon until the dough comes together.
7. Knead the dough on a floured surface for 57 minutes until it becomes smooth and elastic.
8. Place the dough in a lightly oiled bowl and cover it with a damp cloth. Let it rise in a warm place for 3040 minutes.

9. Preheat the oven to 400°F (200°C). Divide the dough into 810 equal pieces and roll each piece into a circle, about 67 inches in diameter.
10. Place the rolled out dough onto a baking sheet lined with parchment paper and bake for 57 minutes until the bread is puffed up and lightly golden.
11. Serve the lamb kebabs with tzatziki sauce and warm pita bread. Enjoy!

Caesar Salad Chicken

Ingredients:

- 1 cup caesar salad dressing
- 1/2 cup ground parmesan cheddar
- Bread garnishes (discretionary)
- 2 boneless, skinless chicken breast,
- Salt and pepper
- Olive oil
- 8 cups cleaved romaine lettuce

Directions:

1. The oven should be heated to 375°F.
2. The chicken bosoms should be seasoned with salt and pepper.

3. In a large skillet, heat the oil to mediumhigh.
4. Add a sprinkle of olive oil to the skillet and singe the chicken bosoms for 23 minutes for each side, until seared.
5. Bake the chicken breasts for 20 to 25 minutes, or until they are cooked through.
6. Allow the chicken bosoms to cool for 5 minutes before cutting them into strips.
7. Combine the chopped romaine lettuce, Parmesan, and Caesar dressing in a large bowl.

Butter And Garlic Steak

Ingredients:

- 2 garlic cloves, minced
- 1 tablespoon new parsley, slashed
- 1 tablespoon new thyme leaves, slashed
- 2 rib eye steaks, around 1 inch thick
- Salt and pepper, to taste
- 4 tablespoons unsalted margarine, at room temperature

Directions:

1. In a cast-iron skillet, heat the oil to medium high.
2. On both sides, generously season the rib eye steaks with salt and pepper.

3. When the skillet is hot, add the steaks and cook for around 34 minutes on each side, or until they are caramelized and singed.
4. While the steaks are cooking, blend the mellowed margarine, minced garlic, parsley, and thyme in a little bowl.
5. After the steaks have reached the desired doneness, remove them from the skillet and allow them to rest for five minutes on a cutting board.
6. Each steak should have garlic herb butter on top.
7. Serve up your delicious Garlic Herb Butter Steak and enjoy its flavor!

Pork Tenderloin With Mustard Crust

Ingredients:

- 1 tablespoon fresh thyme leaves

- 1 teaspoon salt

- 1/2 teaspoon black pepper

- 2 tablespoons olive oil

- 1 pound pork tenderloin

- 2 tablespoons Dijon mustard

- 2 cloves garlic, minced

Directions:

1. Preheat the oven's temperature to 400°F (200°C).

2. Mix the Dijon mustard, minced garlic, fresh thyme, salt, and pepper in a small bowl. To make a mustard crust, thoroughly combine.
3. With paper towels, dry the pork tenderloin. Salt and black pepper should be used to season the pork tenderloin.
4. In a skillet that is oven safe, heat the olive oil over medium high heat. When the oil is hot, add the pork tenderloin and sear it for two to three minutes on each side, or until a golden brown crust forms, on all sides.
5. After taking the skillet off the heat, evenly cover the top and sides of the pork tenderloin with the mustard crust mixture.
6. Put the oven on before adding the skillet containing the pork tenderloin. Roast for 15 to 20 minutes, or until the pork achieves an internal temperature of 145°F (63°C).
7. The pork tenderloin should be moved to a chopping board after taking the pan out of the

oven. Before slicing, give it five minutes to rest.
8. The pork tenderloin should be cut into medallions and served right away.

www.ingramcontent.com/pod-product-compliance
Lightning Source LLC
LaVergne TN
LVHW010226070526
838199LV00062B/4732